The Adventures of
BOBBY
The Big Red Bus
A Day in the Rain

By Steven Donaldson
Illustrations by Lisa Blary

In London, England, there are big, red, shiny double-decker buses carrying passengers all over the city.

"Good morning, Bobby, are you fully charged for the day?" asked Henry the mechanic.

"Good morning, Henry! Yes, I am, and ready to go!" said Bobby.

Because Bobby is an electric bus and needs a charge every morning so he can run all-day.

Andy the conductor joins Bobby at the front
of the bus station as it begins to rain.

Bobby is very excited
as he has never seen rain before.

Bobby hears the sound of raindrops hitting
the road pitter-patter and cannot wait to get
out and pick up the passengers.

Andy and Bobby leave the bus station to pick up their first passengers of the day.

Bobby drives by the park. Children are playing in the rain having fun, jumping in the puddles, and laughing out loud.

"Looks like a lot of fun," says Bobby to the kids.

Splash, splash, splash!

Andy points out interesting sights to the passengers such as the Millennium Wheel which goes around and around and shows tourists the beautiful city of London.

Bobby is driving down
the road in the rain.

Suddenly a large tree branch breaks off
a tree and falls into the road!

"Crash" is the loud sound the branch
makes as it hits the road.

"Oh no!" shouts Bobby to the
passengers

Bobby tries to stop but it is too late and
he runs over the tree branch.

Andy gets off the bus to look at the fallen branch and hears a hissing sound coming from the tyre.

"Oh dear," says Bobby, "It sounds like I have a flat tyre! Am I in trouble, Andy?" asks Bobby.

"Bobby, it was an accident and not your fault at all," says Andy.

Andy gets on the phone with another conductor Claire with her bus Beverly, who is near by to pick up Bobby's passengers.

"Hi, Claire, it's Andy. We have a flat tyre, can you and Beverly stop by and pick up the passengers so they can continue on their journey?"

"Great," says Andy, "See you later. Let me call the tow truck to come and change the tyre."

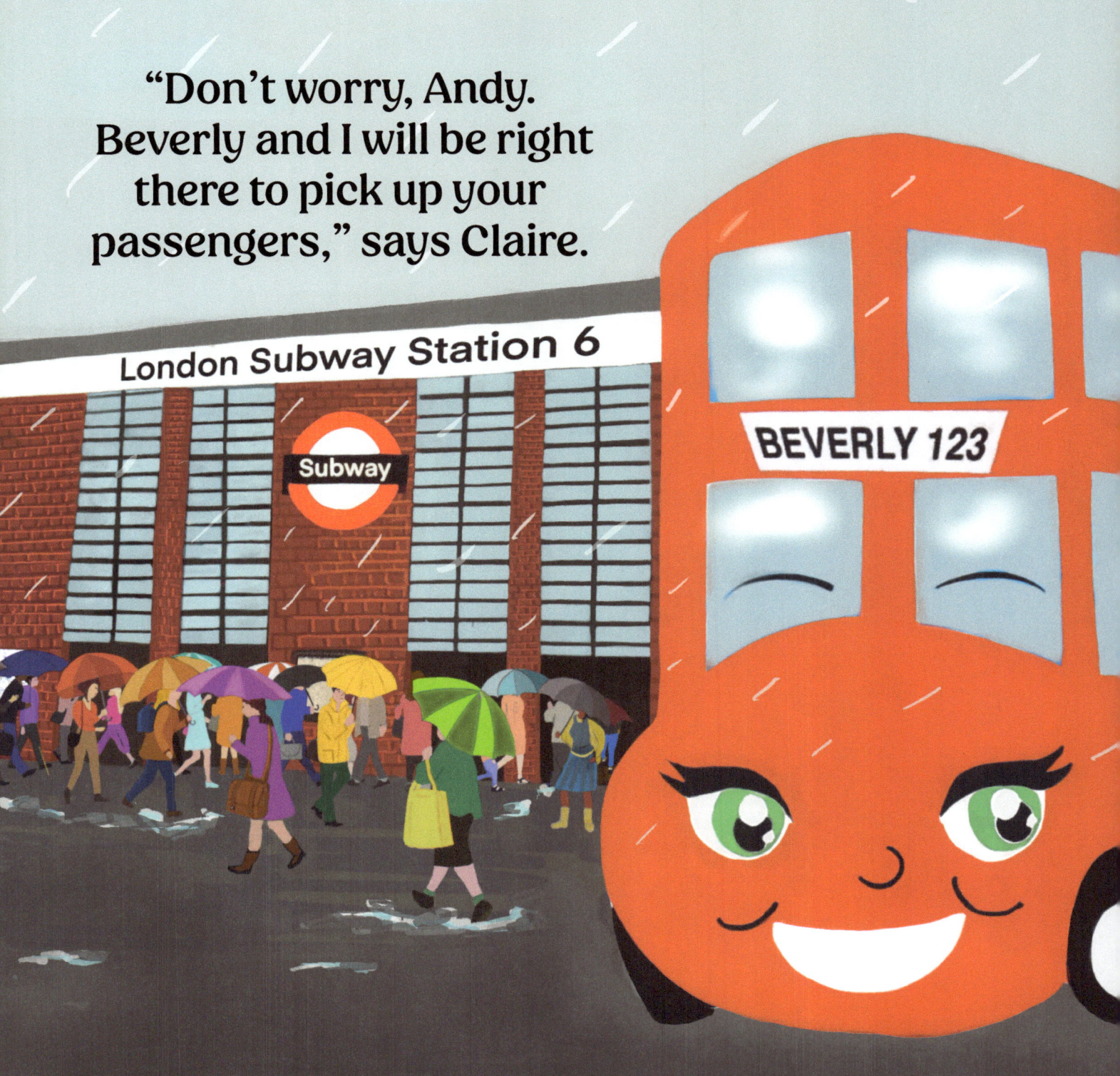

Beverly and Claire arrive to pick up the passengers.

"Are you okay, Bobby?" asks Beverly.

"Thank you, Beverly. I am now that you are here to pick up the passengers," says Bobby.

"Remember what they taught us in bus school? We are part of a team and we are all here to help each other," says Beverly.

"Thanks again, Beverly. You are right. I will see you later at the bus station," says Bobby.

The rain finally stops and the tow truck arrives with Markus and Mo, the two bus mechanics.

Mo and Markus place the orange and white safety cones around the back and side of the bus to warn other drivers to be careful and drive slowly.

Markus and Mo then go to fetch a new tyre for Bobby.

Andy walks up to Markus and Mo who have a new tyre for Bobby.

"Hi, fellas," says Andy.

"Hi, Andy, I have a brand new tyre for Bobby," says Mo.

"Hi, Andy and I will have the old flat tyre off in a jiffy so you can be on your way," says Markus.

This is teamwork.

Bobby is driving back to the bus station with Andy after dropping off the last passengers and the rain has stopped.

Bobby drives by the park. The sky brightens up and the sun begins to shine.

Suddenly a rainbow appears in the sky. Bobby shouts out to Andy.

"Wow, my first rainbow, how beautiful is that?"

Bobby stares at the rainbow with a big smile on his face!

Bobby is in the bus station and it is 8.30 at night. Bobby is ready for bed, as he is very tired.

"What an interesting day you had today, Bobby," says Vincent, the night manager.

"Yes, I saw rain for the first time, I got a flat tyre and all my friends came to help me, and at the end of the day a beautiful rainbow came out to say hi to the world."

"Well, tomorrow will be another exciting and wonderful day," says Vincent.

"Yes, it really is a beautiful world out there," says Bobby.

A large blanket comes down from the ceiling covering Bobby, as Bobby falls asleep.

Bobby is dreaming of his next adventure.

The End

BOBBY: He is innocent, brave, strong, optimistic, always seeing the bright side of things.

Bobby believes every day is a new adventure.

Bobby loves children and all the passengers.

Bobby loves the outdoors, sun, and rain, and never complains.

Bobby is best friends with Beverly and Brian.

BEVERLY: Beverly is Bobby's best friend. She is reliable, honest, friendly, and fearless.

Beverly believes she can do anything that the other buses can do.

Beverly is big-hearted and is always willing to go to help others in need.

BETTIE: She is the gossip of the group and likes to know everything that is happening at the bus station.

Bettie is friendly with all the buses, even Barry.

Bettie is a fast talker and prefers taking it slow and easy on the streets of London and does not like to rush from bus stop to bus stop.

BILLY: He is the perfectionist of the group who always tries to do everything by the book.

Billy always tells the other buses how to do things and gets anxious when everything is not perfect.

Billy's best friend is Bobby and Bobby helps comfort Billy when things don't always go smoothly.

BARRY: He is boastful and a little mean sometimes and likes to cause trouble.

Barry is a little lazy and does not like going out into the cold and rain.

Barry prefers staying in the bus station telling the other buses how great he is.

BRIAN: He is the joker of the group always telling corny jokes and always making Bobby laugh.

Brian does not take life seriously and instead lives each day as it comes.

Brian never gets upset and sees the bright side of any bad situation.

Brian likes to drive faster between the bus stops and sometimes unfortunately drives right past the passengers.

About the Author

STEVEN DONALDSON

Steven is a writer and owner of THE BIG RED BUS COMPANY in Hollywood, CA. Steven has experienced first hand the positive and genuine love for these Iconic red London Double Decker buses. Steven decided, based on his years of experience, to create a character that children worldwide could love and enjoy. And so he wrote a bedtime story. Here it is "THE ADVENTURES OF BOBBY THE BIG RED BUS."

For more BOBBY books see:
THE ADVENTURES OF BOBBY THE BIG RED BUS
"THE JOURNEY BEGINS" available online.

WWW.BOBBYBIGREDBUS.COM

About the Illustrator

LISA BLARY

Lisa is a French artist living in Los Angeles. Lisa dedicates this book to her daughter Sarah and all the children of the World that love bedtime stories.

Copyright © 2023 Stephen M Donaldson

All rights reserved. This book or any portion thereof may not be reproduced or used in any manner whatsoever without the express written permission of the publisher except for the use of brief quotations in a book review.

ISBN: 978-1-7379747-4-1 First Printing, 2024